# Great Works Instructional Guides for Literature

# Green Eggs and Ham

A guide for the book by Dr. Seuss
Great Works Author: Torrey Maloof

## Image Credits

Shutterstock (cover. p. 20, p. 39, p. 49, p. 56, p. 63, p. 69–70)

## Standards

© 2007 Teachers of English to Speakers of Other Languages, Inc. (TESOL)
© 2007 Board of Regents of the University of Wisconsin System. World-Class Instructional Design and Assessment (WIDA)
© Copyright 2010. National Governors Association Center for Best Practices and Council of Chief State School Officers. All rights reserved.

---

### Shell Education
5301 Oceanus Drive
Huntington Beach, CA 92649-1030
http://www.shelleducation.com
**ISBN 978-1-4258-8965-4**
© 2015 Shell Educational Publishing, Inc.

The classroom teacher may reproduce copies of materials in this book for classroom use only. The reproduction of any part for an entire school or school system is strictly prohibited. No part of this publication may be transmitted, stored, or recorded in any form without written permission from the publisher.

# Table of contents

**How to Use This Literature Guide** .................................... 4
    Theme Thoughts .................................................. 4
    Vocabulary ...................................................... 5
    Analyzing the Literature ......................................... 6
    Reader Response ................................................. 6
    Guided Close Reading ............................................ 6
    Making Connections .............................................. 7
    Language Learning ............................................... 7
    Story Elements .................................................. 7
    Culminating Activity ............................................ 8
    Comprehension Assessment ........................................ 8
    Response to Literature .......................................... 8

**Correlation to the Standards** ........................................ 8
    Purpose and Intent of Standards ................................. 8
    How to Find Standards Correlations .............................. 8
    Standards Correlation Chart ..................................... 9
    TESOL and WIDA Standards ....................................... 10

**About the Author—Dr. Seuss** ......................................... 11
    Possible Texts for Text Comparisons ............................ 11

**Book Summary of *Green Eggs and Ham*** ............................... 12
    Cross-Curricular Connection .................................... 12
    Possible Texts for Text Sets ................................... 12

**Teacher Plans and Student Pages** .................................... 13
    How to Read the Book ........................................... 13
    Pre-Reading Theme Thoughts ..................................... 14
    Section 1: Meet the Characters ................................. 15
    Section 2: Repetition and Rhyme ................................ 24
    Section 3: Powerful Punctuation! ............................... 33
    Section 4: Don't Give Up! ...................................... 42
    Section 5: Try Something New! .................................. 51

**Post-Reading Activities** ............................................ 60
    Post-Reading Theme Thoughts .................................... 60
    Culminating Activity: Get Creative! ............................ 61
    Comprehension Assessment ....................................... 64
    Response to Literature: Being Brave ............................ 66

**Writing Paper** ...................................................... 69

**Answer Key** ......................................................... 71

# Introduction

# How to Use This Literature Guide

Today's standards demand rigor and relevance in the reading of complex texts. The units in this series guide teachers in a rich and deep exploration of worthwhile works of literature for classroom study. The most rigorous instruction can also be interesting and engaging!

Many current strategies for effective literacy instruction have been incorporated into these instructional guides for literature. Throughout the units, text-dependent questions are used to determine comprehension of the book as well as student interpretation of the vocabulary words. The books chosen for the series are complex and are exemplars of carefully crafted works of literature. Close reading is used throughout the units to guide students toward revisiting the text and using textual evidence to respond to prompts orally and in writing. Students must analyze the story elements in multiple assignments for each section of the book. All of these strategies work together to rigorously guide students through their study of literature.

The next few pages describe how to use this guide for a purposeful and meaningful literature study. Each section of this guide is set up in the same way to make it easier for you to implement the instruction in your classroom.

## Theme Thoughts

The great works of literature used throughout this series have important themes that have been relevant to people for many years. Many of the themes will be discussed during the various sections of this instructional guide. However, it would also benefit students to have independent time to think about the key themes of the book.

Before students begin reading, have them complete the *Pre-Reading Theme Thoughts* (page 14). This graphic organizer will allow students to think about the themes outside the context of the story. They'll have the opportunity to evaluate statements based on important themes and defend their opinions. Be sure to keep students' papers for comparison to the *Post-Reading Theme Thoughts* (page 60). This graphic organizer is similar to the pre-reading activity. However, this time, students will be answering the questions from the point of view of one of the characters in the book. They have to think about how the character would feel about each statement and defend their thoughts. To conclude the activity, have students compare what they thought about the themes before they read the book to what the characters discovered during the story.

## How to Use This Literature Guide (cont.)

### Vocabulary

Each teacher reference vocabulary overview page has definitions and sentences about how key vocabulary words are used in the section. These words should be introduced and discussed with students. Students will use these words in different activities throughout the book.

On some of the vocabulary student pages, students are asked to answer text-related questions about vocabulary words from the sections. The following question stems will help you create your own vocabulary questions if you'd like to extend the discussion.

- How does this word describe _____'s character?
- How does this word connect to the problem in this story?
- How does this word help you understand the setting?
- Tell me how this word connects to the main idea of this story.
- What visual pictures does this word bring to your mind?
- Why do you think the author used this word?

At times, you may find that more work with the words will help students understand their meanings and importance. These quick vocabulary activities are a good way to further study the words.

- Students can play vocabulary concentration. Make one set of cards that has the words on them and another set with the definitions. Then, have students lay them out on the table and play concentration. The goal of the game is to match vocabulary words with their definitions. For early readers or English language learners, the two sets of cards could be the words and pictures of the words.

- Students can create word journal entries about the words. Students choose words they think are important and then describe why they think each word is important within the book. Early readers or English language learners could instead draw pictures about the words in a journal.

- Students can create puppets and use them to act out the vocabulary words from the stories. Students may also enjoy telling their own character-driven stories using vocabulary words from the original stories.

# Introduction

## How to Use This Literature Guide (cont.)

### Analyzing the Literature

After you have read each section with students, hold a small-group or whole-class discussion. Provided on the teacher reference page for each section are leveled questions. The questions are written at two levels of complexity to allow you to decide which questions best meet the needs of your students. The Level 1 questions are typically less abstract than the Level 2 questions. These questions are focused on the various story elements, such as character, setting, and plot. Be sure to add further questions as your students discuss what they've read. For each question, a few key points are provided for your reference as you discuss the book with students.

### Reader Response

In today's classrooms, there are often great readers who are below average writers. So much time and energy is spent in classrooms getting students to read on grade level that little time is left to focus on writing skills. To help teachers include more writing in their daily literacy instruction, each section of this guide has a literature-based reader response prompt. Each of the three genres of writing is used in the reader responses within this guide: narrative, informative/explanatory, and opinion. Before students write, you may want to allow them time to draw pictures related to the topic. Book-themed writing paper is provided on pages 69–70 if your students need more space to write.

### Guided Close Reading

Within each section of this guide, it is suggested that you closely reread a portion of the text with your students. Page numbers are given, but since some versions of the books may have different page numbers, the sections to be reread are described by location as well. After rereading the section, there are a few text-dependent questions to be answered by students.

Working space has been provided to help students prepare for the group discussion. They should record their thoughts and ideas on the activity page and refer to it during your discussion. Rather than just taking notes, you may want to require students to write complete responses to the questions before discussing them with you.

Encourage students to read one question at a time and then go back to the text and discover the answer. Work with students to ensure that they use the text to determine their answers rather than making unsupported inferences. Suggested answers are provided in the answer key.

# How to Use This Literature Guide (cont.)

## Guided Close Reading (cont.)

The generic open-ended stems below can be used to write your own text-dependent questions if you would like to give students more practice.

- What words in the story support . . . ?
- What text helps you understand . . . ?
- Use the book to tell why _____ happens.
- Based on the events in the story, . . . ?
- Show me the part in the text that supports . . . .
- Use the text to tell why . . . .

## Making Connections

The activities in this section help students make cross-curricular connections to mathematics, science, social studies, fine arts, or other curricular areas. These activities require higher-order thinking skills from students but also allow for creative thinking.

## Language Learning

A special section has been set aside to connect the literature to language conventions. Through these activities, students will have opportunities to practice the conventions of standard English grammar, usage, capitalization, and punctuation.

## Story Elements

It is important to spend time discussing what the common story elements are in literature. Understanding the characters, setting, plot, and theme can increase students' comprehension and appreciation of the story. If teachers begin discussing these elements in early childhood, students will more likely internalize the concepts and look for the elements in their independent reading. Another very important reason for focusing on the story elements is that students will be better writers if they think about how the stories they read are constructed.

In the story elements activities, students are asked to create work related to the characters, setting, or plot. Consider having students complete only one of these activities. If you give students a choice on this assignment, each student can decide to complete the activity that most appeals to him or her. Different intelligences are used so that the activities are diverse and interesting to all students.

# Introduction

## How to Use This Literature Guide (cont.)

### Culminating Activity

At the end of this instructional guide is a creative culminating activity that allows students the opportunity to share what they've learned from reading the book. This activity is open ended so that students can push themselves to create their own great works within your language arts classroom.

### Comprehension Assessment

The questions in this section require students to think about the book they've read as well as the words that were used in the book. Some questions are tied to quotations from the book to engage students and require them to think about the text as they answer the questions.

### Response to Literature

Finally, students are asked to respond to the literature by drawing pictures and writing about the characters and stories. A suggested rubric is provided for teacher reference.

## Correlation to the Standards

Shell Education is committed to producing educational materials that are research and standards based. As part of this effort, we have correlated all of our products to the academic standards of all 50 states, the District of Columbia, the Department of Defense Dependents Schools, and all Canadian provinces.

### Purpose and Intent of Standards

Standards are designed to focus instruction and guide adoption of curricula. Standards are statements that describe the criteria necessary for students to meet specific academic goals. They define the knowledge, skills, and content students should acquire at each level. Standards are also used to develop standardized tests to evaluate students' academic progress. Teachers are required to demonstrate how their lessons meet standards. Standards are used in the development of all of our products, so educators can be assured they meet high academic standards.

### How to Find Standards Correlations

To print a customized correlation report of this product for your state, visit our website at http://www.shelleducation.com and follow the online directions. If you require assistance in printing correlation reports, please contact our Customer Service Department at 1-877-777-3450.

# correlation to the standards (cont.)

## standards correlation chart

The lessons in this book were written to support the Common Core College and Career Readiness Anchor Standards. The following chart indicates which lessons address the anchor standards.

| Common Core College and Career Readiness Anchor Standard | Section |
| --- | --- |
| **CCSS.ELA-Literacy.CCRA.R.1**—Read closely to determine what the text says explicitly and to make logical inferences from it; cite specific textual evidence when writing or speaking to support conclusions drawn from the text. | Guided Close Reading Sections 1–5; Story Elements Sections 1–4; Language Learning Section 2 |
| **CCSS.ELA-Literacy.CCRA.R.2**—Determine central ideas or themes of a text and analyze their development; summarize the key supporting details and ideas. | Analyzing the Literature Sections 1–5; Story Elements Sections 1, 5; Making Connections Sections 3–4; Post-Reading Theme Thoughts |
| **CCSS.ELA-Literacy.CCRA.R.3**—Analyze how and why individuals, events, or ideas develop and interact over the course of a text. | Analyzing the Literature Sections 1–5; Guided Close Reading Sections 1–5; Story Elements Sections 3–4 |
| **CCSS.ELA-Literacy.CCRA.R.4**—Interpret words and phrases as they are used in a text, including determining technical, connotative, and figurative meanings, and analyze how specific word choices shape meaning or tone. | Vocabulary Sections 1–5 |
| **CCSS.ELA-Literacy.CCRA.R.10**—Read and comprehend complex literary and informational texts independently and proficiently. | Entire Unit |
| **CCSS.ELA-Literacy.CCRA.W.1**—Write arguments to support claims in an analysis of substantive topics or texts using valid reasoning and relevant and sufficient evidence. | Reader Response Sections 1–2; Story Elements Section 4; Post-Reading Response to Literature |
| **CCSS.ELA-Literacy.CCRA.W.2**—Write informative/explanatory texts to examine and convey complex ideas and information clearly and accurately through the effective selection, organization, and analysis of content. | Reader Response Section 3 |
| **CCSS.ELA-Literacy.CCRA.W.3**—Write narratives to develop real or imagined experiences or events using effective technique, well-chosen details and well-structured event sequences. | Reader Response Sections 4–5 |

# Introduction

## Correlation to the Standards (cont.)

### Standards Correlation Chart (cont.)

| Common Core College and Career Readiness Anchor Standard | Section |
|---|---|
| CCSS.ELA-Literacy.CCRA.W.4—Produce clear and coherent writing in which the development, organization, and style are appropriate to task, purpose, and audience. | Post-Reading Response to Literature |
| CCSS.ELA-Literacy.CCRA.L.1—Demonstrate command of the conventions of standard English grammar and usage when writing or speaking. | Language Learning Sections 2–5; Making Connections Section 3; Reader Response Sections 1–5 |
| CCSS.ELA-Literacy.CCRA.L.2—Demonstrate command of the conventions of standard English capitalization, punctuation, and spelling when writing. | Language Learning Sections 1, 3; Making Connections Section 3; Reader Response Sections 1–5 |
| CCSS.ELA-Literacy.CCRA.L.4—Determine or clarify the meaning of unknown and multiple-meaning words and phrases by using context clues, analyzing meaningful word parts, and consulting general and specialized reference materials, as appropriate. | Vocabulary Sections 1–5 |
| CCSS.ELA-Literacy.CCRA.L.5—Demonstrate understanding of figurative language, word relationships, and nuances in word meanings. | Vocabulary Sections 1, 3 |

## TESOL and WIDA Standards

The lessons in this book promote English language development for English language learners. The following TESOL and WIDA English Language Development Standards are addressed through the activities in this book:

- **Standard 1:** English language learners communicate for social and instructional purposes within the school setting.
- **Standard 2:** English language learners communicate information, ideas and concepts necessary for academic success in the content area of language arts.

**Introduction**

## About the Author—Dr. Seuss

Theodor Seuss Geisel, more commonly known as Dr. Seuss, was born on March 2, 1904, in Springfield, Massachusetts. As a young boy, Geisel loved funny stories, drawing, and animals. He grew up near a zoo, which he would visit quite often. Geisel liked to draw the animals he saw there although his animals always looked a little different and strange. Geisel's parents encouraged their son's playful imagination but also taught him the importance of hard work and a good education.

In 1921, Geisel graduated from high school and left for Dartmouth College. There he drew cartoons for the college magazine called *Jack-o-Lantern*. Some of the cartoons were of imaginary animals while others showed people doing silly things.

Geisel graduated from college in 1925 and traveled to England to attend Oxford University where he studied literature. He was going to become a professor, yet Geisel's true passion was still drawing. His friend Helen Palmer told Geisel that he should be drawing for a living. Geisel took her advice and left Oxford. He returned to the United States to try and make his dreams come true. A short time later, Palmer and Geisel were married.

Many different magazines hired Geisel as a cartoonist. Then in 1937, his first book called *And to Think That I Saw It on Mulberry Street* was published under the name Dr. Seuss. Geisel wrote many more books for children over the years. In 1957, a publishing company asked Geisel to write a book for beginning readers. The publisher gave him a list of words to use. The book Geisel wrote became one of his most famous books of all time. It was called *The Cat in the Hat*.

Geisel continued to write children's books and even won the Pulitzer Prize in 1984. In 1990, he published his last book called *Oh, the Places You'll Go!* He passed away the following year. Geisel's famously funny and colorful stories continue to delight readers young and old. More than 600 million copies of his books have been sold worldwide.

## Possible Texts for Text Comparisons

In 1957, Geisel helped establish a new publishing company for children learning to read. The company published *Beginner Books*. Geisel wrote many of these books. They include *The Cat in the Hat*, *Hop on Pop*, *One fish two fish red fish blue fish*, and *Fox in Socks*.

# Introduction

## Book Summary of *Green Eggs and Ham*

"Do you like green eggs and ham?" asks Sam-I-am. Throughout the book, Sam-I-am persistently tries to persuade the character in the black hat to try the peculiar concoction of green eggs and ham. Sam-I-am offers the odd dish in a variety of locations with a long list of different animals all in the hopes of enticing the character in the black hat to try something new. The character in the black hat is stubborn and refuses to give in to Sam-I-am's rhyming and repetitious pleas. That is, until the end of the book. The character in the black hat finally acquiesces to Sam-I-am's request and takes a bite of the strange-looking food only to find that he does indeed like green eggs and ham!

## Cross-Curricular Connection

This book can be used to teach a math unit on counting. Students can count the words in the book, the animals in the book, or the different locations in the book. This book can also be used to teach a unit on healthy eating. Students can discuss what foods are healthy to eat. Or, teachers can use this book to support a science unit on animals. Students can compare and contrast the animals mentioned in the book. Students can also discuss the different animals that lay eggs. Finally, this book can be used in an art unit in which students draw their own odd food concoctions.

## Possible Texts for Text Sets

- Donohue, Moira Rose. *Penny and the Punctuation Bee*. Whitman, Albert & Company, 2010.
- Lyons, Shelly. *If You Were an Exclamation Point*. Capstone Press, 2009.
- _____. *If You Were a Question Mark*. Capstone Press, 2009.
- Petty, Kate. *The Perfect Pop-Up Punctuation Book*. Penguin Young Readers Group, 2006.
- Truss, Lynne. *Eats, Shoots & Leaves: Why, Commas Really Do Make a Difference!* Putnam Juvenile, 2006.

or (being persistent)

- Brown, Peter. *You Will Be My Friend!* Little Brown Books for Young Readers, 2011.
- Schoberl, Elisabeth. *When Donkeys Fly!* North-South Books, Inc., 2007.
- Silverman, Erica. *Mrs. Peachtree's Bicycle*. Simon & Schuster Books for Young Readers, 1996.
- Woodworth, Deborah. *Determination: The Story of Jackie Robinson*. The Child's World, Inc., 1998.

or (trying new things)

- Hoban, Russell. *Bread and Jam for Frances*. HarperCollins Publishers, 1986.
- Watt, Mélanie. *Scaredy Squirrel*. Kids Can Press, Limited, 2008.
- Willems, Mo. *Today I Will Fly!* Disney-Hyperion, 2007.

# Introduction

## How to Read the Book

Each section of this instructional guide contains lessons and activities to help students gain an understanding of the story in a variety of ways. A summary of each section is given below to be a guide each time you share this book with your class.

### Section 1: Meet the Characters

This section focuses on the two main characters in the book. Understanding the different personality traits of the two characters will enhance the young readers' comprehension of the book and its themes.

### Section 2: Repetition and Rhyme

This section focuses on the use of rhyming words and the repetition of certain phrases in the book. As you read through the book this time, look at the words that rhyme and the phrases that are repeated. The vocabulary for this section focuses on some of the more notable rhyming words.

### Section 3: Powerful Punctuation!

This section focuses on the use of punctuation in the book. As you read the book through this time, point out the various punctuation marks. Focus primarily on the question marks and the exclamation points.

### Section 4: Don't Give Up!

This section focuses on the theme of persistence. Sam-I-am is persistent and does not give up when the character in the black hat refuses to try the odd food. As you read through the book, allude to Sam-I-am's determination.

### Section 5: Try Something New!

This section focuses on the importance of being brave and adventurous and the theme of trying new things. The character in the black hat tries something new and likes it. As you read the book, allow students to express their thoughts and feelings on trying new things.

**Introduction**

Name _____

# Pre-Reading Theme Thoughts

**Directions:** Read each statement. Draw a picture of a happy face or a sad face. The face should show how you feel about the statement. Then, use words to say why you feel this way.

| Statement | How Do You Feel? | Why Do You Feel This Way? |
|---|---|---|
| Sometimes people are not happy. | | |
| It is a good thing not to give up. | | |
| It is important to try new things. | | |
| It is okay to change your mind. | | |

**Teacher Plans—Section 1**
**Meet the Characters**

# Vocabulary Overview

Key words and phrases from this section are provided below with definitions and sentences about how the words are used in the story. Introduce and discuss these important vocabulary words with students. If you think these words or other words in the story warrant more time devoted to them, there are suggestions in the introduction for other vocabulary activities (page 5).

| Word or Phrase | Definition | Sentence about Text |
|---|---|---|
| **I** (p. 3) | the person who is speaking or writing | **I** think you will enjoy the book *Green Eggs and Ham*. |
| **do** (p. 9) | to perform an action or activity; also used as a helping verb to create a question | **Do** you think the character in the black hat will eat green eggs and ham? |
| **not** (p. 9) | used to make a word or group of words negative (to show dislike) | The character in the black hat does **not** like Sam-I-am. |
| **like** (p. 9) | to enjoy something | Do you **like** to eat green eggs and ham? |
| **may** (p. 28) | used to say that something is possible | The character in the black hat **may** like the green eggs and ham. |
| **let me be** (p. 34) | a way of telling someone to leave you alone | The character in the black hat tells Sam-I-am to "**let me be**" because he does not want to be bothered anymore. |
| **you see** (p. 39) | a way of saying you hope someone else understands what you are saying | I think Sam-I-am can solve the problem **you see**. |
| **so you say** (p. 53) | a way of saying you do not really believe what someone is saying | Sam-I-am cannot solve the problem, **so you say**. |
| **try** (p. 53) | to make an effort to do something | Sam-I-am wants the character in the black hat to **try** the green eggs and ham. |
| **thank you** (p. 62) | a way of telling someone you are grateful for something he or she has done or given | **Thank you** for reading *Green Eggs and Ham*. |

**Meet the characters**

Name _____

# Vocabulary Activity

**Directions:** Draw lines to complete the sentences.

| Beginnings of Sentences | Endings of Sentences |
|---|---|
| At the beginning of the story, the character in the black hat | does **not** give up. |
| Sam-I-am thinks the character in the black hat | is happy and says **thank you**. |
| The character in the black hat is not happy | **may** like green eggs and ham. |
| Sam-I-am keeps trying and | does not **like** Sam-I-am. |
| At the end of the story, the character in the black hat | and tells Sam-I-am "**let me be**"! |

**Directions:** Answer this question.

1. Why does Sam-I-am want the character in the black hat to **try** green eggs and ham?

_____

_____

16   #40002—Instructional Guide: Green Eggs and Ham   © Shell Education

*Teacher Plans—Section 1*
*Meet the Characters*

# Analyzing the Literature

Provided below are discussion questions you can use in small groups, with the whole class, or for written assignments. Each question is written at two levels so you can choose the right question for each group of students. For each question, a few key points are provided for your reference as you discuss the book with students.

| Story Element | Level 1 | Level 2 | Key Discussion Points |
|---|---|---|---|
| Character | Is Sam-I-am a happy or angry character? | Describe Sam-I-am. | Students should describe Sam as happy and silly. He has a big smile on his face throughout the book. Sam is also confident. He proudly states his name out loud and on a sign, and he boldly asks the character in the black hat to try eating green eggs and ham. He does not get discouraged as the story moves along. He stays positive until the very end. |
| Character | How does the character in the black hat change in the story? | How do you think Sam-I-am feels about the way the character in the black hat changes in the story? | In the beginning of the story, the character in the black hat states with disgust that he does not like Sam-I-am. He is stubborn in his refusal to try green eggs and ham and his anger, impatience, and frustration with Sam-I-am seem to increase as the story moves along. The character changes when he agrees to try the food. By the end of the story, his demeanor changes to one of happiness, excitement, and gratitude. |
| Setting | Where is the character in the black hat when he first sees Sam-I-am? | Tell what you know about the setting at the very beginning of the story. | Students should note that the character in the black hat is sitting in a chair reading. Students should discuss the various places he could be (home, park, town). They should note that he is reading and appears to be annoyed that Sam-I-am is disturbing him and invading his space. |
| Plot | What does the character say when Sam-I-am asks him to try green eggs and ham? | Why does the character in the black hat say he does not like green eggs and ham? | The character in the black hat tells Sam-I-am that he does not like green eggs and ham. Students should discuss reasons why the character would say that he does not like them when he has yet to try them. He may think he does not like them because they are green or maybe because he wants Sam-I-am to leave. |

Meet the characters

Name _____

# Reader Response

**Think**

In the story, there are two main characters. There is the character in the black hat and Sam-I-am. Think about which character is your favorite.

**Opinion Writing Prompt**

Write about your favorite character. Describe the reasons you like this character.

_____
_____
_____
_____
_____
_____
_____
_____

Name _____

Meet the Characters

# Guided Close Reading

Closely reread pages 1–12, where the character in the black hat first meets Sam-I-am.

**Directions:** Think about these questions. In the space below, write ideas or draw pictures as you think. Be ready to share your answers.

❶ Use the pictures to describe Sam-I-am.

❷ Use the text to describe how the character in the black hat feels about Sam-I-am.

❸ Based on the text and pictures, how does the character in the black hat feel about green eggs and ham?

© Shell Education · #40002—Instructional Guide: Green Eggs and Ham · 19

**Meet the characters**

Name _____

# Making connections—Feelings

**Directions:** The character in the black hat is **not** happy in the beginning of the book. Sam-I-am is happy. Think about times when you are **not** happy. Then think about times when you are happy. List these times on the chart below.

| Not Happy | Happy |
|---|---|
|   |   |

Name _____

Meet the characters

# Language Learning—Dialogue

**Directions:** Write what you think the character in the black hat would say to Sam-I-am if he did like green eggs and ham. Then write what Sam-I-am would say.

"_____

_____

_____

_____"

_____,

## says the character in the black hat.

"_____

_____

_____

_____"

_____,

## says Sam-I-am.

© Shell Education #40002—Instructional Guide: Green Eggs and Ham 21

**Meet the characters**

Name _____

# Story Elements—Characters

**Directions:** Pick two words from the Word Bank that describe Sam-I-am. Write the words on the lines below to finish the sentences. Then draw a picture of Sam-I-am.

### Word Bank

| happy | yellow | proud |
|-------|--------|-------|
| short | nice   | fun   |

Sam-I-am is _____.

Sam-I-am is _____.

Name _____

Meet the characters

# Story Elements—Setting

**Directions:** This story takes place in many silly settings. Draw a picture of you eating green eggs and ham in a silly setting.

# Teacher Plans—Section 2
## Repetition and Rhyme

## Vocabulary Overview

Key words and phrases from this section are provided below with definitions and sentences about how the words are used in the story. Introduce and discuss these important vocabulary words with students. If you think these words or other words in the story warrant more time devoted to them, there are suggestions in the introduction for other vocabulary activities (page 5).

| Word | Definition | Sentence about Text |
| --- | --- | --- |
| **house** (p. 19) | a building in which people live | Sam-I-am is standing in a **house**. |
| **mouse** (p. 19) | a very small animal with a pointed nose and a long, thin tail | There is a little **mouse** in the house. |
| **box** (p. 22) | a container that has four sides, a bottom, and a cover | The **box** is hanging from a tree. |
| **fox** (p. 22) | a small wild animal that has a long pointy nose and a bushy tail | There is a pink **fox** in the box. |
| **train** (p. 33) | a group of railroad cars that travel on a track | The **train** is going fast on the track. |
| **rain** (p. 38) | water that falls in drops from clouds in the sky | The character in the black hat gets wet in the **rain**. |
| **goat** (p. 42) | a small animal with horns, a short tail, and straight hair | The **goat** has two horns. |
| **boat** (p. 44) | a small vessel for traveling on water | The **boat** in the book is yellow. |

**Name** _____

*Repetition and Rhyme*

# Vocabulary Activity

**Directions:** Choose at least two words from the story. Draw a picture that shows what these words mean. Label your picture.

### Words from the Story

| house | box | train | boat |
|-------|-----|-------|------|
| mouse | fox | rain  | goat |

**Directions:** Answer this question.

1. What word from the book rhymes with **house**?
_____
_____
_____

# Teacher Plans—Section 2
# Repetition and Rhyme

## Analyzing the Literature

Provided below are discussion questions you can use in small groups, with the whole class, or for written assignments. Each question is written at two levels so you can choose the right question for each group of students. For each question, a few key points are provided for your reference as you discuss the book with students.

| Story Element | Level 1 | Level 2 | Key Discussion Points |
|---|---|---|---|
| Character | What is the name of the character in the red hat? | Why do you think the character is called Sam-I-am and not just Sam? | Students should discuss that Sam-I-am is used for rhyming purposes but also that it says a lot about Sam-I-am's character. He is proud and outgoing. He knows who he is. |
| Character | What does the character in the black hat mean when he says he will not eat green eggs and ham anywhere? | Why does the character in the black hat tell Sam-I-am that he will not eat the green eggs and ham "anywhere"? | The character in the black hat does not like green eggs and ham and is trying to make a point that no matter where Sam-I-am puts the food he will not eat it. There is no place in the world where he will try it. Be sure to touch on the point that the word *anywhere* also rhymes with the line "hear or there." |
| Setting | Where does Sam-I-am think the character in the black hat and the fox should eat the green eggs and ham? | Why do you think Sam-I-am pairs a fox with a box? | Point out that fox rhymes with box. Ask students to find other examples where the names of the location and partner chosen by Sam-I-am rhyme. |
| Plot | What does the character in the black hat do after he tries the green eggs and ham? | Describe how the character in the black hat reacts after trying the green eggs and ham. | The character in the black hat is excited. He proudly proclaims that he does like green eggs and ham. He repeats that he likes them. He says they are good and that he will eat them anywhere. He is thankful for Sam-I-am and even says "thank you" twice. |

Name _____

**Repetition and Rhyme**

# Reader Response

### Think

Think about other books you have read that use rhymes. Did you like those books? Do you like rhymes?

### Opinion Writing Prompt

Write about how you feel about rhymes. Describe why you like them or don't like them.

**Repetition and Rhyme**

Name _____

# Guided Close Reading

Closely reread page 46, where the character in the black hat says all the places he will not eat green eggs and ham.

**Directions:** Think about these questions. In the space below, write ideas or draw pictures as you think. Be ready to share your answers.

❶ Which words are used over and over again on this page?

❷ Based on the text and the pictures, how do you know the character in the black hat does not like green eggs and ham?

❸ Based on the text, is there some place where the character in the black hat would like to eat green eggs and ham?

Name _____

Repetition and Rhyme

# Making connections—Animals

**Directions:** Sam-I-am talks about three animals in the story. There is a mouse in a house, a fox in a box, and a goat on a boat. List some more animals and then think of a word that rhymes with each animal.

| Animal | Rhyming Word |
|---|---|
|  |  |
|  |  |
|  |  |

© Shell Education · #40002—Instructional Guide: Green Eggs and Ham

**Repetition and Rhyme**

Name _____

# Language Learning—Adjectives

**Directions:** There are three animals in the story. Draw a picture of each one. Then, write at least one adjective about each animal. An adjective is a word that describes something.

mouse

_____

_____

fox

_____

_____

goat

_____

_____

Name _____

**Repetition and Rhyme**

# Story Elements—Plot

**Directions:** Fill in what happened next.

➡ Sam-I-am asks, "Do you like green eggs and ham?"

_____
_____
_____
_____
_____
_____

➡ The character in the black hat tries green eggs and ham.

_____
_____
_____
_____
_____
_____

**Repetition and Rhyme**

Name _____

# Story Elements—Setting

**Directions:** Draw a map of where the story *Green Eggs and Ham* takes place. Be sure to include these places:

- house
- box
- tree
- boat

**Teacher Plans—Section 3
Powerful Punctuation!**

## Vocabulary Overview

Key words and phrases from this section are provided below with definitions and sentences about how the words are used in the story. Introduce and discuss these important vocabulary words with students. If you think these words or other words in the story warrant more time devoted to them, there are suggestions in the introduction for other vocabulary activities (page 5).

| Word or Phrase | Definition | Sentence about Text |
|---|---|---|
| **do** (p. 9) | to perform an action or activity; also used as a helping verb to create a question | **Do** you think the character in the black hat will eat green eggs and ham? |
| **would** (p. 14) | used to talk about a possible situation | **Would** the character in the black hat eat the food in a house? |
| **here** (p. 14) | in this place; at this location | The character in the black hat will not eat them **here**. |
| **there** (p. 14) | in that place; at that location | The character in the black hat will not eat them **there**. |
| **anywhere** (p. 16) | in, at, or to any place | The character in the black hat says he will not eat green eggs and ham **anywhere**. |
| **could** (p. 26) | used to say that something is possible | **Could** the character in the black hat eat the food with a mouse? |
| **let me be** (p. 34) | a way of telling someone to leave you alone | The character in the black hat tells Sam-I-am to "**let me be**" because he does not want to be bothered anymore. |
| **say** (p. 36) | used to express surprise or shock | **Say!** The character in the black hat did eat them. |

**Powerful Punctuation!**

Name _____

# Vocabulary Activity

**Directions:** Each of these sentences is taken from the story written by Dr. Seuss. Cut apart these sentence strips. Put the sentences in order. Use the story to help you.

"If you will **let me be**, I will try them."

"**Say!** I will eat them ANYWHERE!"

"**Would** you like them in a house?"

"**Could** you, would you, with a goat?"

"I **do** not like that Sam-I-am!"

# Teacher Plans—Section 3
# Powerful Punctuation!

## Analyzing the Literature

Provided below are discussion questions you can use in small groups, with the whole class, or for written assignments. Each question is written at two levels so you can choose the right question for each group of students. For each question, a few key points are provided for your reference as you discuss the book with students.

| Story Element | Level 1 | Level 2 | Key Discussion Points |
|---|---|---|---|
| Character | Does the character in the black hat like Sam-I-am at the beginning of the story? | How does the character in the black hat feel about Sam-I-am at the beginning of the story? | The character in the black hat states with disgust that he does not like Sam-I-am. At this point in the book, Sam-I-am has only passed by the character in the black hat holding a sign and proudly saying his name. It is not clear why the character in the black hat does not like Sam-I-am. Perhaps something happened before the story begins. |
| Character | How does the character in the black hat feel about Sam-I-am at the end of the story? | How has the character in the black hat's feelings toward Sam-I-am changed by the end of the story? | The character in the black hat has gone from disliking Sam-I-am at the beginning of the story to being very grateful toward Sam-I-am. He tells him thank you with an exclamation point and then says thank you again. He also smiles at him and puts his arm around him. It now appears that the two are friends. |
| Setting | Where is the character in the black hat when he tries green eggs and ham? | Describe the setting in which the character in the black hat tries the green eggs and ham. | The character in the black hat is in water when he finally tries the food. He may be in a lake or an ocean. He is wet and tired and surrounded by a variety of different creatures that are all staring at him waiting for him to eat the food. |
| Plot | Why does Sam-I-am keep asking the character in the black so many questions? | What evidence shows that Sam-I-am wants the character in the black hat to try green eggs and ham? | Sam-I-am asks the character in the black hat fifteen questions during the story. This shows that he is persistent and determined to get the character in the black hat to try the unusual food. |

Powerful Punctuation! Name _____

# Reader Response

### Think
Think about question marks and exclamation points. How do you know when to use the right one?

### Informative/Explanatory Writing Prompt
Describe what you do when you have to use a question mark or exclamation point. What steps do you take to make sure you use the right one?

_____
_____
_____
_____
_____
_____
_____
_____
_____

Name _____

**Powerful Punctuation!**

# Guided close Reading

Closely reread page 33, where Sam-I-am is trying to get the character in the black hat to eat green eggs and ham on a train.

**Directions:** Think about these questions. In the space below, write ideas or draw pictures as you think. Be ready to share your answers.

❶ What kind of punctuation do you see on this page?

❷ What question does Sam-I-am ask the character in the black hat on this page?

❸ What is Sam-I-am excited about on this page? How do you know?

**Powerful Punctuation!**   Name _____

# Making Connections— Asking Questions

**Directions:** Sam-I-am asks the character in the black hat lots of questions. What two questions would you ask the character in the black hat if you could talk to him? Be sure to put a question mark at the end of each question.

1. _____
_____
_____
_____
_____

2. _____
_____
_____
_____
_____

Name _____

**Powerful Punctuation!**

# Language Learning—Exclamations!

**Directions:** Write at least three sentences about the story. Each one must end with an exclamation point.

**Powerful Punctuation!**  Name _____

# Story Elements—Plot

**Directions:** Think about the story *Green Eggs and Ham*. Answer the questions in sentences.

1. What is the first question Sam-I-am asks the character in the black hat?

   _____
   _____
   _____
   _____

2. What does the character in the black hat do after he eats the green eggs and ham?

   _____
   _____
   _____
   _____

Name _____

**Powerful Punctuation!**

# Story Elements—Characters

**Directions:** Sam-I-am asks the character in the black hat many questions. What if the character in the black hat asked Sam-I-am a question? What do you think he would ask? Write the question below. Draw a picture to go with your question.

_____
_____
_____
_____
_____ ?

# Teacher Plans—Section 4
## Don't Give Up!

## Vocabulary Overview

Key words and phrases from this section are provided below with definitions and sentences about how the words are used in the story. Introduce and discuss these important vocabulary words with students. If you think these words or other words in the story warrant more time devoted to them, there are suggestions in the introduction for other vocabulary activities (page 5).

| Word | Definition | Sentence about Text |
|---|---|---|
| **house** (p. 19) | a building in which people live | Sam-I-am is standing in a **house**. |
| **box** (p. 22) | a container that has four sides, a bottom, and a cover | The **box** is hanging from a tree. |
| **car** (p. 26) | a vehicle that has four wheels and an engine and carries passengers | Sam-I-am is driving a **car**. |
| **tree** (p. 28) | a usually large plant that has a thick wooden stem and branches | The **tree** in the book is on a hill. |
| **train** (p. 33) | a group of railroad cars that travel on a track | The **train** is going fast on the track. |
| **dark** (p. 36) | having very little or no light | It is **dark** in the tunnel. |
| **rain** (p. 38) | water that falls in drops from clouds in the sky | The character in the black hat gets wet in the **rain**. |
| **boat** (p. 44) | a small vessel for traveling on water | The **boat** in the book is yellow. |

Name _____

Don't Give Up!

# Vocabulary Activity

**Directions:** Complete each sentence below. Use one of the words listed.

**Words from the Story**

| boat | car | train |

1. A _____ floats in water.

2. A _____ travels on tracks.

3. A _____ drives on roads.

**Directions:** Answer this question.

4. Why does it get **dark** when the characters ride on the train?

_____
_____
_____
_____

**Teacher Plans—Section 4**
**Don't Give Up!**

## Analyzing the Literature

Provided below are discussion questions you can use in small groups, with the whole class, or for written assignments. Each question is written at two levels so that you can choose the right question for each group of students. For each question, a few key points are provided for your reference as you discuss the book with students.

| Story Element | Level 1 | Level 2 | Key Discussion Points |
|---|---|---|---|
| Character | How does the character in the black hat respond to each of Sam's suggestions? | Why does the character in the black hat repeat what Sam-I-am says instead of simply saying no? | The character in the black hat repeats what Sam-I-am says but adds the word *not*. Students should discuss that the character in the black hat wants to make it clear to Sam-I-am that he does not care where or with whom the green eggs and ham are served, he will not eat them because he does not like them. |
| Setting | Does the story take place in one spot or many different spots? | Why does the story take place in so many different locations? | The story takes place in a variety of different make-believe locations. Sam-I-am is trying different locations such as a house, a train, a car, a boat, and even underwater in an attempt to convince the character in the black hat to try green eggs and ham. |
| Plot | How does Sam-I-am get the character in the black hat to try the green eggs and ham? | What else could Sam-I-am have done to get the character in the black hat to try the green eggs and ham? | Sam-I-am offers green eggs and ham to the character in the black hat in many different locations with many different partners. He is persistent and does not give up. Students may suggest other locations or partners that Sam-I-am could have included or they may suggest something entirely different such as Sam-I-am taking a bite first. |
| Plot | Why does the character in the black hat finally try the green eggs and ham? | What does the character in the black hat want in exchange for trying the green eggs and ham? | The character in the black hat agrees to try green eggs and ham because he is tired of dealing with Sam-I-am. He agrees to eat the food if Sam-I-am will leave him alone. Students may note that while Sam-I-am does not give up, the character in the black hat essentially does give up and gives in to Sam-I-am's request. |

Name _____

Don't Give Up!

# Reader Response

## Think
Think about a time you had to try really hard. You kept trying and trying. You did not give up.

## Narrative Writing Prompt
Write about a time that you did not give up. What did you do? Why did you keep trying?

**Don't Give Up!**

Name _____

# Guided Close Reading

Closely reread pages 46–53, where Sam-I-am is trying to get the character in the black hat to eat green eggs and ham.

**Directions:** Think about these questions. In the space below, write ideas or draw pictures as you think. Be ready to share your answers.

❶ Use the book to describe the different ways Sam-I-am tries to get the character in the black hat to eat green eggs and ham.

❷ Use the text to tell how Sam-I-am does not give up after the character in the black hat says he does not like green eggs and ham.

❸ Based on the events, what else could Sam-I-am have done to get the character in the black hat to try green eggs and ham?

Name _____

**Don't Give Up!**

# Making Connections— Encouraging Others

**Directions:** Sam-I-am does not give up. He keeps trying. Make a poster to hang on a wall at your school that will encourage your friends to keep trying and not give up.

Don't Give Up!

Name _____

# Language Learning—Plural Nouns

**Directions:** The bold word in each sentence is a noun. Rewrite each sentence changing the bolded noun to a plural noun.

1. He will not eat them with a **fox**.

   _____

2. He will not eat them with a **goat**.

   _____

3. He will not eat them with a **mouse**.

   _____

Name _____

Don't Give Up!

# Story Elements—Plot

**Directions:** The character in the black hat feels differently at different parts of the story. Cut out the boxes at the bottom of the page. Glue them in the chart in the order that the character in the black hat feels them.

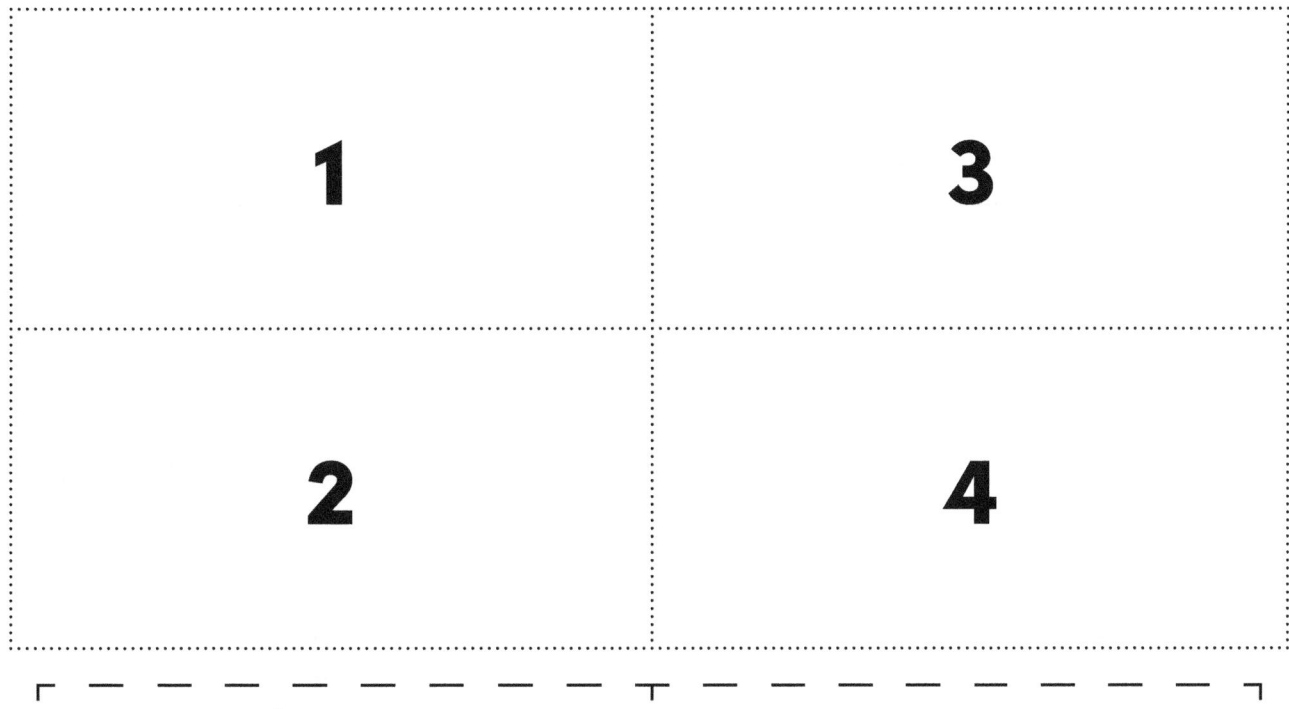

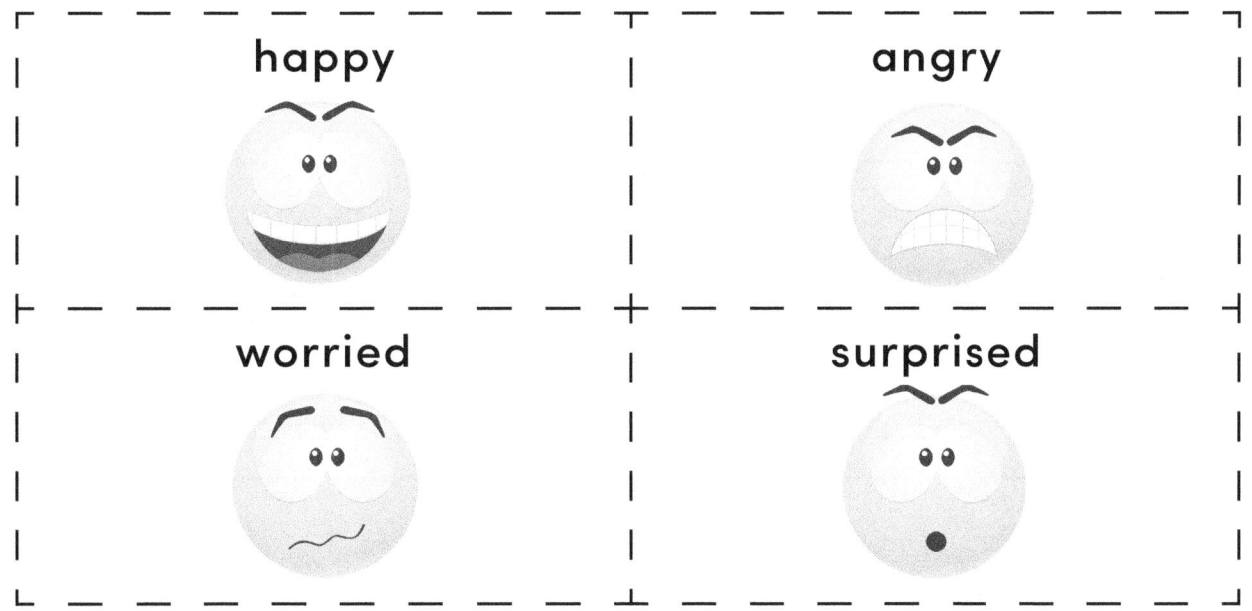

© Shell Education          #40002—Instructional Guide: Green Eggs and Ham          49

Don't Give Up!

Name _____

# Story Elements—Characters

**Directions:** At the beginning of the story, the character in the black hat does not like Sam-I-am. At the end of the story, he thanks Sam-I-am. Do you think the two characters become friends? Describe your prediction on the lines below.

_____
_____
_____
_____
_____
_____
_____
_____
_____
_____

**Teacher Plans—Section 5**
**Try Something New!**

## Vocabulary Overview

Key words and phrases from this section are provided below with definitions and sentences about how the words are used in the story. Introduce and discuss these important vocabulary words with students. If you think these words or other words in the story warrant more time devoted to them, there are suggestions in the introduction for other vocabulary activities (page 5).

| Word | Definition | Sentence about Text |
| --- | --- | --- |
| like (p. 10) | to enjoy something | Do you **like** to eat green eggs and ham? |
| green (p. 10) | having the color of grass and plants | The eggs and ham in the book are **green**. |
| eggs (p. 10) | hard-shelled ovals from birds that are eaten as food | The **eggs** in the book are green. |
| ham (p. 10) | meat from a pig | The **ham** in the book is green. |
| them (p. 12) | used to refer to certain people, animals, or things | The character in the black hat says he does not like **them**. |
| eat (p. 22) | to take food into your mouth and swallow it | The character in the black hat does not want to **eat** green eggs and ham. |
| may (p. 28) | used to say that something is possible | The character in the black hat **may** like the green eggs and ham. |
| will (p. 28) | to say that something is going to happen in the future | The character in the black hat says he **will** try the green food. |
| see (p. 28) | to notice or become aware of something | The character in the black hat says that Sam-I-am will **see** that he does not like green eggs and ham. |
| try (p. 53) | to make an effort to do something | Sam-I-am wants the character in the black hat to **try** the green eggs and ham. |

**Try Something New!**

Name _____

# Vocabulary Activity

**Directions:** Practice your writing skills. Write at least two sentences using words from the story.

### Words from the Story

| green | eggs | ham |
|-------|------|-----|
| may   | like | eat |

_____
_____
_____
_____
_____
_____

**Directions:** Answer this question.

1. At the beginning of the book, did you think the character in the black hat would try the green eggs and ham?

_____
_____
_____
_____

# Teacher Plans—Section 5
## Try Something New!

## Analyzing the Literature

Provided below are discussion questions you can use in small groups, with the whole class, or for written assignments. Each question is written at two levels so you can choose the right question for each group of students. For each question, a few key points are provided for your reference as you discuss the book with students.

| Story Element | Level 1 | Level 2 | Key Discussion Points |
|---|---|---|---|
| Character | Describe the two main characters. | Compare and contrast the two main characters. | Sam-I-am is cheerful, proud, and persistent. Students may also say he is friendly and fun as he is trying to persuade the character in the black hat to try something new. The character in the black hat is also persistent. He repeatedly tells Sam-I-am no. His personality differs from Sam-I-am in that he is angry and frustrated. He does not want to try new things and wants to be left alone. |
| Character | How do you think the character in the black hat feels right before he eats the green eggs and ham? | Have you ever felt the way the character in the black hat feels right before he eats the green eggs and ham? | The character in the black hat is tired from all of Sam-I-am's antics and looks very worried about trying the food. He is wearing a frown and his eyes look sad. He is nervous about eating the green food. Students should discuss times in which they were nervous about trying something new. |
| Plot | What color are the eggs and ham? | Why would the author make the eggs and ham green? | Students should discuss that it is unusual for eggs and ham to be green. Students may think the food looks unappetizing or disgusting. It is important to note here the idea of not judging a book by its cover. The food may look unappealing but the character in the black hat likes the food after he tries it. |
| Plot | What does Sam-I-am want? | Why does Sam-I-am want the character in the black hat to try green eggs and ham? | Sam-I-am wants the character in the black hat to try green eggs and ham because he thinks he will like the unusual food. Direct students toward discussing the importance of trying new things even if you think you may not like it. |

**Try Something New!**

Name _____

# Reader Response

### Think

In the book, the character in the black hat tries to eat something new. He does not think he will like it but he does. Think about a time you had to try and do something new.

### Narrative Writing Prompt

Write about a time that you tried to do something new. Maybe it was trying a new sport. Or maybe it was trying to play a new game. What did you do? Did you like it?

_____
_____
_____
_____
_____
_____
_____
_____
_____

Name _____

**Try Something New!**

# Guided Close Reading

Closely reread pages 54–62, where the character in the black hat tries the green eggs and ham.

**Directions:** Think about these questions. In the space below, write ideas or draw pictures as you think. Be ready to share your answers.

❶ Use the text and pictures to tell why the character in the black hat is finally going to try green eggs and ham.

❷ Look at the picture on page 57. How do you think the character in the black hat is feeling? What is he thinking?

❸ Based on the book, describe how the character in the black hat feels about green eggs and ham after he eats them.

Try Something New!

Name _____

# Making Connections— Trying New Foods

**Directions:** It is important to try new things. The character in the black hat tries a new type of food and likes it. Try one new food each day this week. In the chart below, write what kind of food you tried. Draw a smiley face if you liked it. Draw a sad face if you did not like the food.

| Day of the Week | Food | 😊 😟 |
|---|---|---|
| Monday | | |
| Tuesday | | |
| Wednesday | | |
| Thursday | | |
| Friday | | |

Name _____

**Try Something New!**

# Language Learning— Alphabetical Order

**Directions:** Green eggs and ham are strange foods to try. Below is a list of other silly and strange food. Rewrite the list putting the food in alphabetical order.

## Word Bank

| pink pancakes | blue bananas | yellow yams |
| --- | --- | --- |
| gray grapes | orange oatmeal | maroon milk |

1. _____

2. _____

3. _____

4. _____

5. _____

6. _____

**Try Something New!**

Name _____

# Story Elements—Setting

**Directions:** *Green Eggs and Ham* is set in a fantasy or pretend world. If you had to create a fantasy setting, what would it look like? Draw a picture of your fantasy setting below.

Name _____

**Try Something New!**

# Story Elements—Characters

**Directions:** The character in the black hat changes his mind at the end of the story. He tries the green eggs and ham and likes them. Think of a time when you have changed your mind. Write a sentence about it. Then, draw a picture to go with your sentence.

**Post-Reading Activities**

Name _____

# Post-Reading Theme Thoughts

**Directions:** Choose a main character from *Green Eggs and Ham*. Pretend you are that character. Draw a picture of a happy face or a sad face to show how the character would feel about each statement. Then use words to explain your picture.

**Character I Chose** _____

| Statement | How Does the Character Feel? 😊 ☹️ | Why Does the Character Feel That Way? |
|---|---|---|
| Sometimes people are not happy. | | |
| It is a good thing not to give up. | | |
| It is important to try new things. | | |
| It is okay to change your mind. | | |

**Post-Reading Activities**

# Culminating Activity: Get Creative!

**Directions:** Work with students to help them choose one or more of the following activities to complete. For the first activity, there is a story template on page 62. Make a few copies of this page for each student. Students can then staple the pages together to make their books. For the second activity, there is a survey sheet on page 63. Have students take the survey home to complete or have them ask older students. When the surveys have been conducted, help students tally the results by making a graph on the board.

## Green Eggs and Ham... and Me!

Imagine that you are a character in the book. Rewrite the story to include yourself. Will you be helping Sam-I-am? Will you try to convince the character in the black hat to try green eggs and ham? Or maybe you will be friends with the character in the black hat. Will Sam-I-am convince you to try the strange food? Have fun with this new story. Be silly and creative!

## How Do You Like Your Eggs?

There are many ways to cook an egg. Which way do you think is the most popular? Let's conduct a survey! Ask five people you know how they like their eggs? Write the answer on the sheet your teacher gives you. Then, work with your classmates to tally all the survey results. Make a graph on the board with your teacher and find the answer to the question.

## We're Poets and We Know It!

Dr. Seuss wrote stories with rhythm and rhyme. A poem is a piece of writing with rhythm that often rhymes. Work with an adult or a friend to write a poem of your own. You will be a poet before you know it.

**Post-Reading Activities**

Name _____

# Green Eggs and Ham... and Me!

Name _____

**Post-Reading Activities**

# How Do You Like Your Eggs? Survey

**Directions:** Ask five people you know how they like their eggs. Place an *X* in the table next to the type of egg they choose.

| Types of Eggs | | #1 | #2 | #3 | #4 | #5 |
|---|---|---|---|---|---|---|
| sunny-side up | | | | | | |
| scrambled | | | | | | |
| hard-boiled | | | | | | |
| deviled eggs | | | | | | |
| other | | | | | | |

© Shell Education     #40002—Instructional Guide: Green Eggs and Ham

**Post-Reading Activities**

Name _____

# Comprehension Assessment

**Directions:** Fill in the bubble for the best answer to each question.

## Meet the Characters

1. Which sentence best describes how the character in the black hat feels about Sam-I-am at the beginning of the story?

    (A) He is happy to see Sam-I-am.
    (B) He is scared of Sam-I-am.
    (C) He loves Sam-I-am.
    (D) He does not like Sam-I-am.

## Repetition and Rhyme

2. Which set of words rhyme?

    (A) mouse, home
    (B) goat, boat
    (C) here, far away
    (D) fox, bag

## Powerful Punctuation!

3. Which sentence below is **not** a question?

    (A) Will you eat green eggs and ham?
    (B) Do you see a fox?
    (C) Would you eat them in a car?
    (D) I like green eggs and ham!

# Comprehension Assessment (cont.)

## Don't Give Up!
4. Describe how Sam-I-am does not give up.

_____

_____

_____

_____

_____

_____

_____

## Try Something New!
5. What shows that the character in the black hat is happy that Sam-I-am helps him try something new?

- (A) "Thank you! Thank you, Sam-I-am!"
- (B) "I would not, could not, with a goat!"
- (C) "I do not like that, Sam-I-am!"
- (D) "So I will eat them in a box."

**POST-READING ACTIVITIES**

Name _____

# Response to Literature: Being Brave

**Directions:** Choose one scene from the book that shows one of the characters being brave. Think about the scene. Draw a picture of the scene below. Then, answer the questions on the next page about your scene. Make sure the picture is neat and in color.

Name _____

Post-Reading Activities

# Response to Literature: Being Brave (cont.)

1. Who is being brave in the scene?

   _____
   _____
   _____
   _____

2. How is the character being brave?

   _____
   _____
   _____
   _____

3. Why is it important to be brave?

   _____
   _____
   _____
   _____
   _____

**Post-Reading Activities**

Name _____

# Response to Literature Rubric

**Directions:** Use this rubric to evaluate student responses.

| Great Job | Good Work | Keep Trying |
|---|---|---|
| ☐ You answered all three questions completely. You included many details. | ☐ You answered all three questions. | ☐ You did not answer all three questions. |
| ☐ Your handwriting is very neat. There are no spelling errors. | ☐ Your handwriting can be neater. There are some spelling errors. | ☐ Your handwriting is not very neat. There are many spelling errors. |
| ☐ Your picture is neat and fully colored. | ☐ Your picture is neat and some of it is colored. | ☐ Your picture is not very neat and/or fully colored. |
| ☐ Creativity is clear in both the picture and the writing. | ☐ Creativity is clear in either the picture or the writing. | ☐ There is not much creativity in either the picture or the writing. |

**Teacher Comments:** _____

_____

_____

_____

Name _____

Writing Paper 1

**Writing Paper 2**

Name _____

The responses provided here are just examples of what students may answer. Many accurate responses are possible for the questions throughout this unit.

**Vocabulary Activity—Section 1:**
**Meet the Characters** (page 16)
- At the beginning of the story, the character in the black hat does not **like** Sam-I-am.
- Sam-I-am thinks the character in the black hat **may** like green eggs and ham.
- The character in the black hat is not happy and tells Sam-I-am "**let me be**!"
- Sam-I-am keeps trying and does **not** give up.
- At the end of the story, the character in the black hat is happy and says **thank you**.

1. He thinks he will like the food.

**Guided Close Reading—Section 1:**
**Meet the Characters** (page 19)
1. Sam-I-am is yellow and white. He has a red hat. He looks happy and proud. He is smiling. He is silly.
2. The character in the black hat does not like Sam-I-am. He says, "That Sam-I-am! That Sam-I-am! I do not like that Sam-I-am!"
3. The character in the black hat looks scared of the green eggs and ham. He may think they will taste bad. He does not want to try them. He says, "I do not like them, Sam-I-am. I do not like green eggs and ham."

**Vocabulary Activity—Section 2:**
**Repetition and Rhyme** (page 25)
1. **Mouse** rhymes with house.

**Guided Close Reading—Section 2:**
**Repetition and Rhyme** (page 28)
1. These words are repeated on page 46: not, like, could, would, will, do, I, and them.
2. He lists all the places he would not eat them and he says he does not like them. In the picture, he is holding his finger up to Sam-I-am to make his point.
3. No, he says he will not eat them anywhere.

**Making Connections—Section 2:**
**Repetition and Rhyme** (page 29)

| cat | hat |
| dog | log |
| lizard | wizard |
| bunny | funny |
| bear | fair |
| snake | lake |

**Story Elements—Section 2:**
**Repetition and Rhyme** (page 31)
- Sam-I-am asks, "Do you like green eggs and ham?" Then, **the character in the black hat says no.**
- The character in the black hat tries green eggs and ham. Then, **he likes them and thanks Sam-I-am.**

**Vocabulary Activity—Section 3:**
**Powerful Punctuation** (page 34)
- "I **do** not like that Sam-I-am!"
- "**Would** you like them in a house?"
- "**Could** you, would you, with a goat?"
- "If you will **let me be**, I will try them."
- "**Say!** I will eat them ANYWHERE!"

**Guided Close Reading—Section 3:**
**Powerful Punctuation** (page 37)
1. There are two exclamation points, one question mark, and two commas.
2. He asks, "Could you, would you, on a train?"
3. Sam is excited about seeing a train because he yells, "A train! A train!" The exclamation points show that he is excited.

**Story Elements—Section 3:**
**Powerful Punctuation** (page 40)
1. Do you like green eggs and ham?
2. He says he likes them. He says all the places he would eat them. He says he would eat them anywhere. He thanks Sam-I-am. He puts his arm around Sam-I-am. He smiles.

**Vocabulary Activity—Section 4:**
**Don't Give Up!** (page 43)
1. A **boat** floats in water.
2. A **train** travels on tracks.
3. A **car** drives on roads.
4. The train travels into a tunnel. It is dark in the tunnel.

**Guided Close Reading—Section 4:**
**Don't Give Up!** (page 46)
1. He tries to get the character to eat green eggs and ham on a boat, with a goat, in the rain, on a train, in the dark, in a tree, in a car, in a box, with a fox, in a house, with a mouse, and here or there.
2. Sam-I-am tells him to "try them" because he may like them. He does not take "no" for an answer.
3. He could have kept listing more animals and more places to try the food.

## Answer Key

**Language Learning—Section 4:**
**Don't Give Up!** (page 48)
1. He will not eat them with **foxes**.
2. He will not eat them with **goats**.
3. He will not eat them with **mice**.

**Story Elements—Section 4:**
**Don't Give Up!** (page 49)
1. angry
2. worried
3. surprised
4. happy

**Guided Close Reading—Section 5:**
**Try Something New!** (page 55)
1. He is tired and wants Sam-I-am to leave him alone. He says he will try them if Sam-I-am will let him be.
2. He looks worried and sick. He is nervous and scared about eating the green eggs and ham. He thinks they will taste bad.
3. He likes green eggs and ham. He says he would eat them anywhere. He says they are so good. He has a big smile on his face and he tells Sam-I-am thank you.

**Language Learning—Section 5:**
**Try Something New!** (page 57)
1. blue bananas
2. gray grapes
3. maroon milk
4. orange oatmeal
5. pink pancakes
6. yellow yams

**Comprehension Assessment** (pages 64–65)
1. D. He does not like Sam-I-am.
2. B. goat, boat.
3. D. I like green eggs and ham!
4. The character in the black hat tells Sam-I-am that he does not like green eggs and ham. But Sam-I-am keeps trying to get the character in the black hat to try them. He asks him to try the green food in different locations and with different animals. The character in the black hat keeps saying no but Sam-I-am does not give up. He keeps telling the character in the black hat to just try the unusual food.
5. A. "Thank you! Thank you, Sam-I-am!"

www.ingramcontent.com/pod-product-compliance
Lightning Source LLC
Chambersburg PA
CBHW082246300426
44110CB00039B/2454